Data Science & Dream Job

Unlock Your Interview Triumph 300+ Proven Tips to Land Your Dream Job

by

Lara Baytol

Hello There!

Thank you for choosing to read my life work. I am Lara Baytol, a passionate accountant and coder who wants to help people with their quest for their dream job. Your support means the world to me. I would love to hear your thoughts on your experience with this book. If you are downloading it from Amazon or not you can always research the title on Amazon and leave a review when it is available. Your reviews on Amazon mean so much and help other individuals learn about survival.

Simply Click Here to share your feedback if you are downloading it from Amazon.

Your support fuels my passion for writing books to help as many people as I can. I look forward to reading your reviews and am truly grateful for your support.

With heartfelt thanks,

Lara Baytol

Table of Contents

Introduction

Embarking on a job hunt in the realm of data science can feel like stepping into a labyrinth, where each turn could either lead you to a dead end or straight to the treasure trove. But worry not, intrepid explorer; this book is your map - perhaps sans the invisible ink and cryptic symbols, but a treasure map, nonetheless. We're here to navigate you through the intricate weave of acing a data science interview, equipping you with the tools, know-how, and panache to snag your dream job. It's a journey, but who says you can't have a bit of fun along the way?

In job interviews, data science sits at a curious crossroads of technical prowess and storytelling finesse. The industry's rapid growth has fostered an equally swift evolution in how its gatekeepers assess potential candidates. It's no longer just about showcasing your technical muscles; your future employer expects you to narrate the tale of data, transforming numbers and patterns into compelling stories that drive decisions. This book dives into this unique blend, ensuring you're well-armed.

Think of this as the prep talk before the big game. We're not just here to cram your head full of Python code, machine learning algorithms, or statistical models (although, don't worry, we've got plenty of that in-store). Instead, we're focusing on molding you into the kind of candidate who knows their stuff and how to communicate it effectively, troubleshoot on the fly, and dazzle interviewers with a blend of confidence and humility. It's about becoming a well-rounded data science Jedi, as much at ease with technical challenges as articulating your thought process.

We're going to kick things off by laying the groundwork by discussing what makes the data science landscape so exhilarating yet challenging. It's a bit like being told you're about to explore a new planet—exciting, yes, but also slightly intimidating. Understanding the terrain is crucial before you start plotting your course.

Following that, we'll unpack the toolkit every aspiring data scientist needs. And no, we're not just talking about beefing up your programming skills or getting cozy with data manipulation tools - though we'll cover that in spades. We're also delving into the soft skills that often need more spotlight but can make or break your interview. Think of them as the secret sauce that gives your data science steak its sizzle.

Then, it's onto the nitty-gritty of resumes and cover letters, crafting them so that they don't just whisper but shout, "I'm the one you've been looking for!" from the pile. It'll be like giving your application a jetpack and a laser guide—precision-targeted and impossible to ignore.

Of course, what would a journey be without challenges? The Data Science Interview Process can be a Hydra, multi-headed, and intimidating. Still, with our strategies, you'll be ready to take on each head, whether technical puzzles or the dreaded behavioral questions. It's all about preparation, understanding what's coming, and having a quiver full of responses ready to fire.

With your arsenal well-stocked, we'll thrust you into case studies and projects where theory meets practice. It's showtime, demonstrating that you know your stuff and can apply it in real-world, data-drenched scenarios. This step is where the rubber meets the road, where all your hard work crystallizes into dazzling displays of your prowess.

And once you've dazzled them? That's when the negotiation dance begins. Getting the offer is a victory, but it's not the endgame. We'll guide you through evaluating that offer and employing tactics to ensure that when you finally shake hands (or bump elbows, as modern times may dictate), you've secured a job that's right for you at the compensation you deserve.

Finally, landing the job isn't the finale. We're also looking at what comes next—those crucial first days and months when you begin to carve out your niche. It's about hitting the ground running, continuous learning, and career growth. Data science is an ever-evolving field, and so too should your career within it.

So, consider this your invitation to embark on a thrilling journey. By the end of it, you won't just be walking into a data science interview, ready to face the music. You'll be conducting the orchestra, confident in your ability to turn the complex symphony of data science into a harmonious melody that resonates with interviewers and employers alike. Let's get started, shall we?

Chapter 1:
Understanding the Data Science Landscape

Welcome to the exhilarating world of data science, where tangled webs of information are deftly unraveled, mysteries are solved with a click, and data rather than whims drive decisions. As we delve into the Data Science Landscape, we must grasp not just the 'what' but the 'why' and the 'how' of this dynamic domain. Too often, job seekers jump headfirst into the pool of data science without pausing to understand the waters they're swimming in. The landscape is vast, dotted with opportunities and pitfalls, and knowing the terrain is half the battle won.

The data science journey has been nothing short of a roller coaster (minus the nausea, hopefully). From its humble beginnings to becoming the sexiest job of the 21st century, data science has evolved at a breakneck speed. But don't let the shiny title fool you; this field demands a hefty toolkit of skills, blending a statistician's mathematical prowess with a detective's investigative rigor. Before we dive into the specifics of breaking into this world—such as mastering Python or wrangling datasets—it's crucial to map out the territory. Understanding the evolution of data science helps in appreciating the why behind the what, setting a solid foundation for aspiring data scientists.

But more than that, knowing the history is needed. An accurate data scientist is a rare breed with hard and soft skills. Consider it Sherlock Holmes with a MacBook—deductive reasoning meets coding power. In the labyrinth of data science, being adept at machine learning algorithms or neural networks is just one side of the coin. The other? Explaining your mind-boggling findings to someone who still thinks Python is just a snake. As we explore the critical skills needed for a data scientist in the next segment, remember—it's not just about crunching numbers in solitude; it's about storytelling with data, making the complex accessible, and driving insights that lead to action. So, let's gear up to navigate the dynamic and demanding world of data science. It's going to be quite the adventure.

The Evolution of Data Science

Let's jump into the heart of the matter: The fascinating journey of data science transitioning from a nerdy buzzword into a central career aspiration. If you're eyeing a job in this field, understanding its history isn't just academic—it's practically your secret weapon. Like your favorite vintage wine, data science has an origin story worth sharing at parties (or network events, if that's more your scene).

Once upon a time, before iPhones and Twitter meltdowns, data analysts (the predecessors of data scientists) were holed up in basements, crunching numbers on giant, humming machines. It was the 1960s, and their tools were rudimentary. Fast forward to the 1980s, and statisticians started to get fancy with predictive models. Yet, nobody called it data science—not yet.

The term "data science" itself started gaining momentum in the late '90s, thanks to statisticians pondering over what to call their evolving field. However, the tech explosion in the early 21st century made data science the golden child of the tech industry. Suddenly, there was an ocean of data from social media, e-commerce, and online activity, just waiting to be analyzed.

Here's where it gets juicy. The 2010s saw a massive surge in demand for people who could make sense of big data. As businesses realized the goldmine of insights in their data, they started hunting for these magical beings who could crunch numbers, predict trends, understand machine learning, and even write some code. Enter the era of the data scientist.

Now, let's talk evolution. Initially, data science was all about big data - volume, velocity, and variety. However, as the field matured, it became evident that what truly mattered was the value extracted from this data. This shift in focus marked a significant evolution in data science from a field obsessed with data for data's sake to a crucial aspect of strategic decision-making.

The data scientist's toolkit has also seen dramatic changes. From Python (no, not the snake) and R to machine learning, artificial intelligence, and everything in between, today's data scientists are expected to wield various tools. And guess what? This evolution isn't stopping anytime soon. The next frontier? Automated data science tool. But knowing how to use them effectively is where the human touch remains irreplaceable.

And as for workplaces, they've evolved, too. Data scientists were once the unicorns of techie startups. Now, they're mainstream, employed in sectors ranging from healthcare to finance and even non-profits and government agencies. The demand has skyrocketed to the point where being a data scientist is considered one of the sexiest jobs of the 21st century. Yes, you heard that right, 'sexy.' Who would've thought it?

But with great demand comes great competition. The pathway into data science has become more structured, with degrees and boot camps popping up like daisies. Yet, the essence of becoming a successful data scientist remains the agility to learn and adapt. This field is as much about continuous learning as it is about technical know-how.

And here's a nugget of wisdom for those ready to dive in—understanding the history of data science is not just about knowing the past but about spotting future trends. It's about recognizing that the core of data science—problem-solving, curiosity, and statistical thinking—is timeless. The tools and technologies will keep changing, but these constants remain your North Star.

So, as you prepare for your data science interviews, remember that you're stepping into an evolving role. You're not just a candidate but a pioneer in a field shaping the future. You're the bridge between raw data and actionable insights. And that, my friend, is a heck of a place to be.

In essence, the evolution of data science is a testament to the ever-changing nature of technology and business needs. Data science has come a long way, from basement operations to boardroom strategies. And for those looking to make their mark, understanding this evolution isn't just helpful—it's crucial.

As you move forward, let the history of data science inspire you. It's a field born out of necessity, nurtured by intellectual curiosity, and now indispensable. Your journey in data science might just be beginning, but remember, you're walking a path that many brilliant minds have paved before you. Here's to making your mark in the evolving landscape of data science.

Remember, landing a job in data science is not just about knowing your algorithms or mastering Python. It's about understanding where the field has been and where it's going. It's about recognizing that, at its core, data science is a blend of art and science, requiring technical skills, creativity, and intuition.

To ace that job interview, show them that you're familiar with the latest tools and technologies and understand the big picture. Demonstrate your knowledge of how data science has evolved and how you can contribute to its future growth. After all, the best data scientists are those who not only solve problems but anticipate them, too.

So, as you gear up for the next step in your data science journey, remember this historical perspective. It will set you apart in interviews and prepare you for a fulfilling career in one of the most dynamic fields. After all, who wouldn't want to be part of a story still being written?

Key Skills for a Data Scientist

Now that we've navigated the evolution of data science, it's time to chat about what you'll need in your arsenal to not just survive but thrive in this field. When you think about it, data scientists are a bit like Swiss Army knives—versatile, adaptable, and always ready with the right tool for the job. But what exactly are those tools—or, in our case, skills?

First, let's talk about math and statistics. Now, I know what you're thinking: "Math? I thought I left that back in school!" But trust me, when it comes to data science, these are your bread and butter. Everything from understanding algorithms to making predictions based on data requires a solid grasp of statistical concepts and mathematical reasoning. So, if numbers make you sweaty, it might be time to dive back into the world of means, medians, and modes.

Next up is the biggie: programming skills. If you aim to crack into data science, proficiency in at least one programming language is non-negotiable. Python and R take the lead here, thanks to their simplicity and the plethora of statistical libraries available. But don't just stop at knowing a few commands; understanding how to manipulate data, create visualizations, and apply machine learning algorithms will truly set you apart.

But wait, there's more! You can only talk about data science by mentioning data wrangling. It's like the pre-party before the actual analysis shindig. Much of your time will be spent cleaning, processing, and ensuring data is in tip-top shape for analysis. It's only sometimes glamorous, but hey, someone's got to do it.

Let's not forget about machine learning. Yes, it sounds like a sci-fi movie concept, but it's far from fiction in data science. Understanding the ins and outs of machine learning models is like having a rockstar status in this field. Whether it's supervised or unsupervised learning, being able to build, test, and deploy these models will make employers swoon.

Now, onto something a bit softer but equally crucial: critical thinking and problem-solving. Data science isn't just about crunching numbers and writing code; it's about asking the right questions and finding innovative solutions. It's about looking at a heap of data and seeing the story it tells, the problems it highlights, and the opportunities it unveils.

Communication skills, you ask? Absolutely critical. Gone are the days when data scientists could sit in isolation, cranking out analyses. These days, you need to be able to translate your complex findings into clear, digestible insights that even the most non-technical stakeholders can comprehend. Whether it's through detailed reports, vivid visualizations, or compelling presentations, being able to share your findings effectively is key.

Let's not forget domain expertise. Sure, technical skills are important, but understanding the industry you're working in can be just as valuable. This kind of expertise allows you to make more informed assumptions, ask better questions, and ultimately provide more impactful insights.

And hey, since we're living in an era of big data, let's talk about big data tools. Familiarity with databases, cloud computing, and big data frameworks like Hadoop and Spark can amplify your data science game. Think of it like upgrading from a regular toolbox to a full-blown workshop.

Finally, curiosity and a willingness to learn are perhaps the most timeless skills you can possess. The field of data science is constantly evolving, with new tools, techniques, and theories cropping up constantly. Keeping that spark of curiosity alive will ensure you keep up, innovate, and push boundaries.

As you march forward to becoming a data scientist, remember that each skill is a building block towards your success. It's not about mastering one and ignoring the rest but developing a harmonious blend that makes you stand out. So, whether you're a math wizard, a coding guru, or a storytelling master, there's a place for you in the data science world.

Tackling the journey to becoming a data scientist might seem daunting initially, but it's also profoundly rewarding. Every dataset you dissect, every model you build, and every insight you unearth contributes to a world of data-driven decisions. So yes, the path is strewn with challenges, but the impact you can make is enormous.

So, grab your mathematical shield, programming sword, and analytical helmet and dive into the adventure of data science. You're not just preparing for a job but gearing up to make a difference. And who knows? With the right attitude, a dash of humor, and a ton of hard work, you might land that dream data science job.

Remember, in the land of data science, being a lifelong learner isn't just recommended; it's essential. Every project, analysis, and failed model is an opportunity to learn and grow. So keep at it, stay curious, and who knows—maybe one day, you'll be the one giving advice to the next generation of data scientists.

In conclusion, arming yourself with these critical skills doesn't just prepare you for the technical aspects of being a data scientist; it prepares you for the adventure ahead. Sure, the journey can be complex and filled with ups and downs, but the satisfaction of solving real-world problems with data is unmatched. So, keep building those skills, pushing forward, and, most importantly, enjoy the ride!

Chapter 2:
Building Your Data Science Toolkit

So, you've got a handle on the data science landscape and are all fired up to dive into the nitty-gritty. Before you envision yourself wowing your future employer with tales of data wizardry, let's pause for a hot minute. You'll need to stock your arsenal with the right tools if you're going to knock those interviewers right off their swivel chairs. Think of it as packing for a journey to the center of the data science universe. Your carry-on? A well-stocked data science toolkit.

First things first, let's talk tech chops. You've probably heard whispers (or, let's be honest, full-blown debates) about the coding languages du jour. Python and R are like the bread and butter of data manipulation and analysis, but take your time with just those. An accurate data science Swiss Army knife also gets cozy with SQL for database shenanigans. It isn't shy around more niche picks that might pop up depending on the job. Meanwhile, mastering tools like Jupyter Notebooks, pandas, and TensorFlow isn't just impressive; it's a rite of passage. Remember, the goal here isn't just to list these on your resume but to wield them like a data-slaying hero in your projects and, eventually, in your interviews.

But, and there's always a but, don't think for a second that the journey ends with technical prowess. You'll also need to pack a hefty dose of soft skills. Top of the list? Communication and problem-solving. Explaining complex data concepts to someone still trying to figure out how to work the office coffee machine is an art form. Likewise, staring down a beastly data problem and strategizing your

12

way to a solution requires creativity, persistence, and a touch of stubbornness. These talents might not get their bullet points in a job listing, but they're the secret sauce that'll make you stand out in a crowd of code jockeys.

Required Technical Skills

So, you've decided to plunge into the thrilling world of data science. Kudos! Next up on your checklist? Arming yourself with the technical skills that'll make you stand out among a stacked pile of applicants. Think of this as collecting infinity stones—each skill you acquire amplifies your capabilities, bringing you one step closer to securing that coveted data science gig. And, just like the infinity stones, there's a spectrum of powers you need to master.

First up, programming languages are the bread and butter of data science. The short answer is no if you're wondering whether you need to be a coding wizard. But, the ability to converse with computers in languages like Python or R isn't just impressive; it's essential. Think of these as your Excalibur - without them, you're just a very enthusiastic person in a cape. We won't dive into the nitty-gritty here since that's a saga. However, understanding the basics and manipulating data structures will put you on the right path. And don't forget SQL! It's like the Swiss Army knife for data scientists - instrumental in almost every scenario involving data retrieval and manipulation.

But it doesn't stop at coding. Data science is vast and filled with mysterious tools and technologies. From data manipulation and analysis tools like Pandas and NumPy in Python to data visualization with Matplotlib and Seaborn, each tool adds a layer of polish to your data storytelling skills. And yes, data storytelling is a thing. It's what transforms you from a data analyst into a data whisperer. But let's save the insights on storytelling for a later chapter. For now, focus on getting comfy with these tools. They are your spell book, enabling you to conjure insights from seemingly mundane numbers and figures.

In a nutshell, while the world of data science is as vast as it is fascinating, starting with these technical skills will set you on a journey from being just another candidate to being the candidate. Remember, it's not just about hoarding all the tools and languages you can find. It's about mastering the right ones and knowing how to wield them effectively in the vast, dragon-filled kingdom of data science. Now, gear up and get ready to embark on your quest to conquer the data science interviews with your newfound arsenal!

Programming Languages

So you're trying to nail that data science interview and land the dream job? Fantastic! Let's dive into one of the core weapons in your arsenal: programming languages. Now, don't freak out! I'm here to guide you through this jungle of codes and syntax so you'll come out swinging like a data science ninja.

First things first, Python is the cool kid on the block. Why? Because it's got versatility, baby! Whether you're scrubbing data sets, automating the boring stuff, or building models that predict the future, Python's got your back. It's like that reliable friend who's good at everything and doesn't complain much (read: user-friendly). Don't just take my word for it. You might be asked to pull off some Python magic during your interview. So, get comfortable with libraries like Pandas for data manipulation, NumPy for numerical data, and Matplotlib for some fancy schmancy graphs.

Moving on, we've got R. Think of R as the eccentric professor— it's super detailed and fantastic for statistical analysis. Some might say it's niche, but in the data science world, R is your ticket to deep insights... kind of like those indie films where you learn something profound about life. To shine in an interview, chat up how you've used R for complex statistical models or data visualization. Drop names like ggplot2 or dplyr and watch your interviewer's eyes light up joyfully.

Now, I know what you're thinking. "What about the other languages? There's more to life than Python and R, right?" Absolutely! SQL isn't a traditional programming language, but it's equally important. Imagine SQL as the librarian who knows where every piece of data is stored. You'll need SQL to fetch data, filter it, and perform aggregations that no self-respecting data scientist can live without. Pro tip: Try to weave in how you've used SQL to solve real-world data problems. That's music to an interviewer's ears.

Let's remember Java and Scala, especially if you're eyeing roles in companies that process Big Data (yes, with capital B's). These languages work seamlessly with Apache Hadoop and Spark, like the big, tough bouncers managing data at scale. Mentioning your proficiency in these languages can set you apart if the job description requires considerable data skills.

But here's where it gets spicy—JavaScript. "JavaScript? In data science?" Yes, for those delightful data visualizations and interactive dashboards. Tools like D3.js can make your data dance on the web. While it's not the main dish, adding JavaScript to your recipe can enhance the flavor of your skill set.

Whew, that's a lot, right? Don't sweat it. The trick is not to master all programming languages but to know which one to use and when. It's like being at a buffet; you don't need to eat everything. Pick the dishes that suit the job you're applying for.

During your interview, it's about more than just listing the languages you know. Tell stories about how you've used them to solve problems, create impact, and drive decisions. Interviewers love that stuff. It shows you're not just a coder but a problem-solver who can use these languages to make sense of the data world.

Remember, learning a programming language is like learning to play an instrument. At first, it's all awkward finger placements and strange notes. But with practice, you start making music. The same goes for coding. Start simple, build projects, and soon, you'll compose symphonies of data-driven solutions.

One more thing—stay curious. The tech world evolves faster than a cheetah on a skateboard. Keep experimenting with new languages and technologies. Maybe a new language on the horizon could be the next big thing in data science. Staying updated is vital. Take a deep breath. You've got this! With a solid understanding of programming languages, you're well on your way to impressing at your data science interviews. Remember to sprinkle in your personality and passion for data. After all, your unique blend of skills and enthusiasm will make you stand out.

So, practice those coding skills, work on projects that showcase your abilities, and walk into that interview with confidence. You're not just another candidate; you're a data-slinging, problem-solving wiz gearing up to make a splash in the world of data science.

And remember, the journey doesn't end with getting the job. The world of data science is vast and filled with endless opportunities to grow and learn. Embrace every challenge and continue to sharpen your programming prowess. That way, you're not just securing a job but building a career.

Now, wow them with your programming savvy and get ready to dive into the exciting, ever-changing seas of data science. Best of luck, and may the code be with you!

Data Manipulation and Analysis Tools

So you've got the basics of Python and R down and feel like a programming ninja. Congrats! But before you dive headfirst into that sea of data, you'll need the right snorkel gear—or, in the data science world, the correct data manipulation and analysis tools. These tools are your best friends in making sense of the data deluge, transforming raw data into insights as if by magic (or, you know, skill and hard work).

First up on the list is the omnipresent Excel. Some might scoff at it—"Excel, really? In this age of high-powered computing?" Let's not underestimate this powerhouse. Excel is like the Swiss Army knife for data scientists. It's there for you when you need to slice and dice data quickly without firing up more complex software. Knowing your way around Excel formulas and pivot tables can make or break your data analysis process, especially in the early stages of your career. And let's not forget the awe-inspiring moment when you pull off an Excel function so complex that it leaves colleagues wondering if you're a wizard.

Then, stepping up the game, we have SQL. A solid grasp of SQL is akin to acquiring a key to a vast library. This language allows you to communicate with databases to retrieve, manipulate, and query data efficiently. In interviews, flaunting your SQL skills can prove to employers that you can handle large datasets that Excel might balk at. It's like saying, "Give me your data, any data, and I will make it talk."

Let's remember the specific data manipulation packages within programming languages. If Python is your jam, then Pandas is your go-to. With its DataFrame structure, you can effortlessly filter, aggregate, and transform data for analysis. It's like having a data-wrangling assistant who tidies up messy datasets without breaking a sweat. R enthusiasts are included in the cold, too. With dplyr and tidyr, R becomes a powerful ally in data manipulation, making your analysis smoother than a well-oiled machine.

Visualization tools are the next big thing on your list. They say a picture is worth a thousand words. In data science, a well-crafted visualization is worth a thousand lines of code. Tools like Tableau and PowerBI allow you to turn complex dataset findings into digestible visual stories. This makes your analysis more comprehensible and highlights your ability to communicate complex insights effectively—a skill every employer is hunting for.

For those into more complex analytical tasks, statistical software like SAS, SPSS, or STATA might be your battle gear. While these tools might seem daunting initially, they offer potent functionalities for statistical analysis, which could be a game-changer in your job interview, showcasing your ability to handle in-depth statistical work and hypothesis testing.

Can't decide which tool to master first? Think of it this way: each tool serves a different purpose and excels in distinct scenarios. Your job is to be like a skilled chef, knowing when to use a paring knife and when to bring out the cleaver. The variety in your toolbox can make you a versatile candidate capable of tackling different tasks effectively.

Let's also talk about the elephant in the room—the cloud. Cloud-based tools such as Google's BigQuery or Amazon's Redshift are becoming indispensable in handling big data. Understanding these platforms elevates your data manipulation skills. It prepares you for the future of data science, where cloud computing reigns. Showing off some cloud analytics chops during your interview could put you ahead of the pack.

Of course, knowing your tools is one thing, but showing how you've used them to achieve results is another. Prepare a few anecdotes or examples where a particular tool or combination of tools solved a significant problem or led to a notable insight. Remember, stories stick in people's minds far longer than lists of skills.

Another piece of wisdom: Practice, practice, practice! Just like you can't learn to swim by reading about it, you can only become proficient in these tools if you get your hands dirty. Dive into projects, tinker with datasets, and challenge yourself with real-world problems. This hands-on experience will prepare you for the questions and tasks you might face in interviews.

Let's debunk a common myth: you don't need to master every data manipulation and analysis tool. It's about finding the right tool for the job and knowing it well enough to wield it confidently. Being a jack-of-all-trades but master of none won't cut it when the stakes are high.

Remember, in interviews, it's as much about how you present your skills as it is about the skills themselves. Be prepared to explain not only how you've used these tools but also why you chose them over others and the advantages they offered in your context. This shows thoughtfulness and a strategic approach to problem-solving.

Lastly, stay curious and keep learning. The data science field and the tools and technologies are constantly evolving. What's cutting-edge today might be yesterday's news tomorrow. Keeping up with the latest developments will help you stay relevant and show potential employers that you're committed to your professional growth.

Armed with these tools and the knowledge of how to use them, you're well on your way to acing that data science interview and landing the job. Remember, it's not just about handling data but transforming it into a story the company can use to make informed decisions. So, show them what you've got, and let your data do the talking.

Essential Soft Skills

Let's be honest for a second: knowing your way around Python or being able to whip up a fancy neural network in TensorFlow is awesome. But here's the kicker: if you can only explain some of that jargon to a room full of non-tech folks, you might as well be speaking ancient Greek. That's where soft skills come into play, and boy, do they play hardball in the data science world. Communication is the golden child of soft skills. It's not just about making your work accessible; it's about storytelling. Imagine you've found some groundbreaking insights in your data. Now, can you sell that story to your team, your boss, or even to the non-data scientist who accidentally wandered into your presentation? That's the magic of communication - transforming complex data into compelling stories that drive action.

But wait, there's more! While being a data whisperer is fantastic, if you hit a problem and crumble like a cookie, that's not exactly a recipe for success. Enter problem-solving - the trusty sidekick of communication. Data science is not a walk in the park (or a walk anywhere predictable, really). You'll encounter data that looks tangled in a brush, missing values that play hide and seek, and algorithms that sometimes act like they're in a bad mood. This is where creativity, patience, and a knack for solving puzzles come into their own. Think of it like being a detective, but instead of solving crimes, you're unraveling data mysteries with the sheer power of your wit (and maybe a bit of Python).

You might be thinking, "Great, I've got to be a storyteller and a detective?" Yep, exactly. But here's the thing – developing these soft skills is not just about becoming a better data scientist; it's about becoming a better colleague and, dare we say, a more awesome human being. And let's be honest, in the high-stakes world of data science interviews, being the candidate who can not only talk the tech talk but also walk the people walk will set you apart from the crowd. So, dive into the deep end of communication and problem-solving. You'll find that these skills will not only help you nail your data science interviews but will also equip you for almost anything the data world throws at you. And who knows, you might even have some fun along the way.

Communication

Let's be real, folks. In the grand scheme of landing your dream job in data science, being able to crunch numbers, while impressive, is only half the battle. The other half? Making sure you can talk about those numbers in a way that doesn't put people to sleep. Communication is the bridge between a great data scientist and a great job offer. You're not just a number-cruncher but a storyteller capable of transforming data into compelling narratives that inform decisions. This section dives deep into the art of communication within data science interviews.

Imagine you've just conducted a groundbreaking analysis that could save your company millions. You've got the technical chops and slayed the data dragon, but now comes the real challenge: explaining your findings to a room full of non-technical folks. This, my friends, is where the rubber meets the road. It would help if you transitioned from data scientist to data storyteller. It's not just what you say, it's how you say it.

Every successful data scientist knows that visualization is their best friend. "Show, don't tell" should be your mantra when it comes to interviews. Whether it's during a technical demonstration or a behavioral interview, being able to represent your findings visually is a game-changer. A well-crafted chart or graph can often communicate what words cannot. But beware, it's not just about throwing every cool chart you know into a PowerPoint. It's about choosing the right visual that complements your story.

And speaking of stories, let's talk about tailoring your narrative. Every data-related question or project can be turned into a story with a beginning, a middle, and an end. First, set the stage with the problem you aimed to solve (beginning), then walk through how you approached the problem and tackled it (middle), and finally, unveil the results of your endeavors (end). This structure makes your explanation more straightforward and engaging for your audience.

But here's the thing: even the best stories fall flat if irrelevant to the listener. That's why understanding your audience is crucial. Before you walk into that interview room, do your homework. Learn about the company, its industry, and, if possible, the specific challenges they are facing. This way, you can tailor your answers and stories to hit home, showing them that you're not just skilled but also thoughtful and adaptable.

Let's remember the importance of simplicity. Einstein famously said, "If you can't explain it simply, you don't understand it well enough." Resist the urge to impress with jargon and complexity. It might feel good to flex your technical vocabulary, but if your interviewer needs help to keep up, you've missed the mark. Strive for clarity and simplicity in your explanations. Remember, your goal is to communicate effectively, not to showcase every technical term you know.

Active listening is another critical component of communication that often goes under the radar. It's not just about waiting for your turn to speak; it's about engaging with the interviewer's questions and comments. This means paying close attention, asking clarifying questions, and responding thoughtfully. Active listening can also help you catch nuances and subtleties about the company's culture and priorities, which can be invaluable in tailoring your responses.

Feedback is your friend. Yes, it can be challenging to hear that your presentation skills need work or that you lost your audience halfway through your explanation of predictive analytics. But feedback is a goldmine for improvement. If you have the opportunity, seek feedback from peers or mentors on your communication skills, especially if you can do so in a mock interview setting. It's the quickest way to identify areas for growth and adjust before the real deal.

Don't underestimate the power of practicing out loud. It's one thing to run through the talking points in your head and another to hear them come out of your mouth. You might be surprised at how different something can sound when spoken versus thought. Practice your answers, stories, and especially technical explanations out loud, in front of a mirror, to a friend, or even to a pet. Practice can help refine your wording, pace, and tone, making your delivery more confident and polished.

Empathy is a secret weapon in effective communication. Empathizing with your audience, whether an interviewer or a team of stakeholders, helps you connect more personally. By putting yourself in their shoes, you can better understand their perspectives, anticipate their questions, and address their concerns more effectively. This connection not only makes your communication more effective but also more memorable.

Let's address the elephant in the room: nerves. It's natural to feel nervous, especially when you're passionate about landing a job in data science. However, nerves can wreak havoc on your communication if not managed. Breathing exercises, positive visualization, and remembering that you've prepared can help keep those jitters at bay. Remember, the interviewer wants you to do well, so take a deep breath and show them what you've got.

Clarity over complexity is your mantra when explaining technical projects. You might have tackled the most complex, data-laden project imaginable. Still, you'll retain your audience if you can boil it down to its essence. Start by explaining the goal of your project in one or two sentences before diving into the details. This gives your audience a clear framework to hang onto as you guide them through the complexities of your work.

Adaptability is key. Interviews can be unpredictable. You might be asked to elaborate on something you didn't anticipate, or your interviewer might have a different level of technical expertise than you expected. The ability to pivot and adapt your communication style is invaluable. Depending on the context, this might mean simplifying your language further or providing more detailed explanations.

Lastly, remember that communication is a two-way street. An interview isn't just about answering questions; it's also about engaging in a discussion. Feel free to ask questions to clarify details and show your genuine interest in the position and the company. This proactive engagement demonstrates your enthusiasm, curiosity, and, most importantly, your ability to communicate effectively and professionally.

So there you have it, future data science stars. Sharpening your communication skills can be as crucial as honing your technical abilities when aiming for that dream job. Remember, the data science field isn't just about numbers and algorithms; it's about making sense of those numbers and convincing others of their importance. Nail that, and you're not just a data scientist; you're a data science communicator, and that, my friends, is a winning combination.

Problem-Solving

If there's one workout routine data scientists need to get comfortable with, it's flexing their problem-solving muscles. Imagine problem-solving as the gym membership for your brain specifically tailored for the data science world. You wouldn't walk into a gym and expect to deadlift double your weight on the first day, right? Similarly, honing your problem-solving skills takes time, practice, and the right approach.

First, let me lay it out straight: problem-solving in data science isn't just about crunching numbers (though that's a big part). It's about looking at a messy pile of data and seeing a story or solution. It's the ability to ask the right questions before thinking of the answers. It's like being a detective, but you're solving business or research puzzles instead of crimes.

So, how do you build this skill? Well, it starts with embracing complexity. Please don't shy away from it. When you encounter a dataset or a problem that makes your head spin, that's your cue to dive in, not step back. Each complex problem you tackle will teach you something new, even if you don't solve it completely. It is collecting keys that might unlock future issues.

Next up is the art of breaking down problems. It's all too easy to feel overwhelmed when you're staring down what appears to be a mountain of an issue. The trick here is not to look at the mountain as a big, complex, unhackable problem but to split it into manageable hiking trails. Take that significant problem and break it into smaller parts. Solve each part independently, and suddenly, the mountain seems manageable.

And then, there's the principle of iterative learning. Okay, so you tried solving a problem and failed. Great! No, seriously, failing is a vital part of problem-solving. It's like experimenting with a recipe that could taste better. You learn what doesn't work, tweak your approach, and try again. The iterative process is crucial in data science, as it often leads you to innovative solutions you wouldn't have thought of initially.

Collaboration is another key ingredient. Sure, the stereotype exists of the lone wolf data scientist, headphones in, world out, lost in their code. But some of the best problem-solving comes from bouncing ideas off others. Whether it's with fellow data scientists, stakeholders, or even friends who know nothing about data science, talking through a problem can spark the idea that leads to a breakthrough.

Now, let's talk about tools. Alongside technical skills, problem-solving strategies are essential tools in a data scientist's toolkit. Whether it's a specific algorithm, a way to visualize data differently, or a method for statistical analysis, knowing what's in your toolbox and when to use it is part of the problem-solving process. It's vital to add to this toolkit through learning and experience continually.

Adapting to failure is also part of the journey. No one likes to fail, but in the world of data science, it's a steppingstone to success. Each failure is a lesson, giving you insights into what doesn't work and pointing you closer to what does. The key is to keep going. Remember, every data scientist you admire has faced their fair share of setbacks and failures. It's all part of the process.

Curiosity is your best friend here. The most effective problem solvers are those who are perpetually curious. They're the ones who ask, "What if?" and "Why not?" even when others don't see the point. This relentless curiosity pushes you to explore all avenues of a problem, often leading to more innovative solutions.

Another aspect to consider is the importance of domain knowledge. Understand the context in which you're solving problems. Data doesn't exist in a vacuum; it's affected by countless real-world factors. By understanding the domain, whether it be finance, healthcare, retail, etc., you can better frame problems and tailor your solutions to be more effective.

Let's also remember time management. Practical problem-solving isn't just about finding the right solution but also about doing so promptly. This is where your skills in prioritizing tasks, breaking down problems, and managing resources come into play. Sometimes, a good enough solution now is better than a perfect solution too late.

A sense of resilience is crucial. There will be days when the data doesn't make sense, and your code doesn't do what it's supposed to. It's easy to feel disheartened. However, the resilience to push through these barriers, to keep probing, asking, and trying, sets apart the good data scientists from the great ones.

Finally, remember to celebrate the small wins. Problem-solving in data science is often a marathon, not a sprint. Celebrating the small victories not only boosts morale but also builds confidence. It's a reminder that progress is being made, even one small step at a time.

In conclusion, becoming a master problem solver in data science is no small feat. It requires a blend of technical knowledge, critical thinking, resilience, and never-ending curiosity. But it's also what makes the field so exciting and fulfilling. As you prepare for your data science interviews, remember that every problem solved, big or small, is a step towards becoming the data scientist companies are eager to hire.

So, go ahead and embrace the puzzles that come your way. See them not as obstacles but as opportunities to hone your problem-solving prowess. With each challenge, you're moving closer to acing your interviews and shaping yourself into a data scientist capable of turning complex problems into insightful solutions.

Chapter 3:
Crafting the Perfect Resume and Cover Letter

So, you've got your data science toolkit ready, and your skills are as sharp as a freshly minted Jupyter notebook. But before you can dazzle with your Python prowess or your mastery over machine learning models, there's a humble gateway you need to cross—craft that perfect resume and cover letter. Remember, in the vast ocean of job applicants, your resume is your lifeline that keeps you afloat, and your cover letter is the beacon that guides hiring managers to your light.

Let's start with the resume - think of it less as a laundry list of your life's achievements and more as a highlight reel explicitly tailored for the role you're eyeing. A one-size-fits-all approach might work for your favorite pair of jeans, but when it comes to resumes for data science roles, customization is key.

Now, onto the art of writing an engaging cover letter – it's basically your first date with the employer and first impressions matter. Begin with a hook that grabs attention faster than a neural net learning pattern but keep it professional (save the memes for Twitter). This isn't the time to rehash your resume. Instead, use this space to narrate the story that your bullet points can't. Connect the dots between your past experiences and the job description. Be bold, be confident, and let them know why you're not just another candidate but the candidate. Remember, an engaging cover letter isn't just about flaunting your credentials; it's about showcasing how you can solve their problems with elegance and efficiency.

I can't stress it enough. You must research the company as profoundly as you can. I know you want to apply to as many job offers as possible but prioritize quality over quantity. If you do this right, six job applications with the correct tailored cover letters are better than twenty with a similar cover letter.

As we wrap up this chapter, remember that your resume and cover letter are the dynamic duo that first introduces you to potential employers. They should complement each other, highlighting where you've been and what you've learned, where you hope to go, and how you plan to contribute.

So, before you hit that 'submit' button, make sure your resume and cover letter are as meticulously crafted as the code you plan to bring to your new team. And remember, in the realm of data science, where the competition is stiff and the challenges are exciting, a well-crafted resume and an engaging cover letter can be the algorithms that set you apart from the dataset. Happy crafting!

Tailoring Your Resume for Data Science Roles

So, you're aiming to break into the world of data science, huh? That's fantastic! But I'll tell you a little secret: your resume needs to be as sharp as your analytical skills. You might have crunched numbers faster than you can say "neural networks," but if your resume doesn't showcase that, it's just another document in the pile. Let's dive into how to tailor that resume to stand out in the data science crowd.

First, understand that a one-size-fits-all approach to resumes doesn't cut it in the data science realm. I know I am repeating myself, but I want to ensure you get this because it will make all the difference. You've got to tweak and tune it like a machine-learning model. For starters, zoom in on the job description. Highlight keywords related to technical skills, software, and soft skills. These are your resume's "keywords" – sprinkle them throughout your resume like fairy dust (but more scientifically).

Now, let's talk about structure because, in data science, structure is king. To kick-off with a bang, you must have a summary statement highlighting your achievements and expertise. When you craft it, put yourself in the shoes of an experienced interviewer or easier in the shoes of the CEO.

How?

Well, ask yourself this question:

"If I owned this company, would I like to interview this person (you) based on this summary statement? Based on this resume? based on this cover letter?"

If the answer is no, you must sell yourself better.

I use this technic for everything, even when writing this book. I asked myself if you, yes you, would read it during each step from choosing the book title and outline to proofreading and book cover.

It is always about value.

Suppose the CEO or the interviewer, who has the company's best interest at heart, sees **value** in you on paper. Then congratulations, half the job is already done.

Think of it as your elevator pitch. If your summary doesn't scream, **"I eat data for breakfast,"** you're doing it wrong.

Your experience section should be the meaty part of your resume. But it's not just about listing job duties. Nope, it would help if you quantified your achievements. Did your machine-learning model improve something? By how much? Numbers are your best friends here. They provide a concrete testament to your accomplishments.

Let's remember the projects. In data science, projects can speak volumes about your skills. List relevant projects you've worked on during your courses, personal projects, or previous jobs. Describe what you did, the tech stack, and the outcome. Did you reduce processing time? Increase accuracy? Here's where you show off.

Ah, and skills. You can't just say you're proficient in Python or R and call it a day. Link those skills to experiences or projects where you utilized them. It adds credibility and shows that you're not just throwing in buzzwords for the heck of it.

Now, onto the softer side of things. Data science isn't just about crunching numbers but solving problems. Highlight your problem-solving abilities, your knack for storytelling with data, or how you've communicated complex data insights to non-techy stakeholders. These soft skills are just as necessary as your technical prowess.

Formatting – please keep data clean and professional for the love of data. Choose a readable font, leave enough white space, and organize sections logically. Your resume reflects your data visualization skills. A cluttered, hard-to-read resume? That's a big red flag.

Include a section for education but make it snappy. Yes, your degree matters, but your skills and experience hold more weight in the data science field. So, unless you've got a Ph.D. in a directly relevant field, keep this section brief and to the point.

Certifications can be a goldmine, especially if you're transitioning from another field. Have you completed a course in data analysis or machine learning? Make sure this has its own special spot on your resume. It shows a commitment to self-improvement and a passion for the field.

Let's not underestimate the power of a hobbies or interest's section. It may seem trivial, but it's a gateway to showing off your personality. Are you interested in chess? Highlight how it enhances your strategic thinking. Remember, data science teams look for fit as much as they do for skill.

Another often overlooked section is volunteering. If you've applied your data science skills in a volunteering capacity, it's worth mentioning. It not only shows your ability to apply your skills in the real world but also your commitment to making a difference.

You might be thinking, "Is there space for languages?" In a global economy, the answer is a resounding yes. If you speak multiple languages, it suggests you can work effectively in diverse environments. It is beneficial if the company deals with international markets.

Finally, tailor your resume for each application. Think of it as A/B testing. Minor tweaks can make a big difference in landing that interview. Use the job description as your guide and adjust accordingly. This shows you're not just blasting out generic resumes but genuinely interested in the role.

So, there you have it. Tailoring your resume for data science roles isn't rocket science. Still, it does require thought, attention to detail, and a sprinkle of creativity. Remember, your resume is the first impression you make. Make it count. Show them you're not just another candidate – you're the data scientist they've been searching for.

The Art of Writing an Engaging Cover Letter

Let's dive into something that makes many of us cringe – the cover letter. Now, before you start groaning and thinking about the hundred ways, you'd rather spend your time, let's shift our perspective a bit, shall we? Crafting a cover letter, especially for a data science role, is less about painful formality and more about showcasing your unique story. It's your golden ticket to make a memorable impression outside of the bullet points on your resume.

First things first, let's talk about personalization. Gone are the days of "To Whom It May Concern." If you're applying for a data science job, odds are you're a bit of a detective yourself. Use those research skills to find out the hiring manager's name and, yes, use it. It's a simple move that can immediately set the tone for a more personal connection.

Getting the intro right can be tricky. You want to start strong but sound different from every other candidate. Avoid the snooze-fest of "I'm writing to apply for..." Instead, hook them with something relevant and engaging. Start with a striking fact about the data science field or a project you've tackled that had a significant impact. The goal? Make them eager to read on.

The body of your cover letter is where the magic happens. This is your chance to tell a story that your resume can't – how your skills, projects, and experiences align with the job description and the company's goals and culture. Have you led a project that saved your company time or money? Have you developed a model that improved decision-making? Here's where you dish out the specifics, quantifying your achievements whenever possible.

But wait. Don't just focus on what you've done. Talk about why you're excited about this opportunity. What is it about data science, and this company in particular, that lights your fire? Companies want to hire people who are passionate about what they do, not just looking for a paycheck.

Remember, you're a data scientist—you know the power of data. So, why not use some relevant data or statistics about the company you're applying to? Show them you've done your homework and understand what challenges they face and how you can help tackle them. This level of detail can really set you apart from the crowd.

Onto the closing section—your cover letter's mic drop moment. It's not enough to recap what you've mentioned earlier. The closing should be confident, forward-looking, and still very much you. Maybe suggest an innovative idea for a project you'd love to start or express excitement about contributing to a specific area of their business. Don't divert away from your line of thinking.

I will tell you a funny story. This can apply to both the cover letter and the interview. I was in a final interview six years ago for a high-end job and was going to get this job for a prominent real estate company. It was my dream job.

The interviewer asked me a final question. I was too comfortable, and the question was: 'Where do you see yourself in our company in 5 years?''

I didn't think. I just said that I wanted to own a real estate empire. That wasn't contributing. It was a personal, selfish goal that detracted from all that I was saying.

I asked for feedback as I didn't get the job, and I learned that that last question made the interviewer feel like I didn't have their best interest at heart. Always remember that your contribution and value to the company is crucial. Don't just talk about yourself and your aspirations; always link that to what you can do for the company.

Ah, and the sign-off – it's more important than you might think. "Yours faithfully" might sound like you're penning a letter to a Victorian love interest, not a hiring manager. Keep it professional but modern with a simple "Best regards" or "Sincerely" followed by your name.

Here's a quirky tip: add a P.S. It grabs attention and is a clever way to reiterate something important or add a tidbit you couldn't fit elsewhere. It could be a link to a relevant project or a notable accomplishment you didn't delve into. It's unconventional, sure, but memorable.

Remember that every company and role is different; your cover letter should be, too. Yes, it's more work, but customization is critical. A generic, one-size-fits-all approach is easy to spot and often ends in the "no" pile.

Now, for the elephant in the room: length. This isn't the time to pen your autobiography. Keep it concise – a page is plenty. You aim to whet their appetite, not feed them a five-course meal. Say enough to intrigue them, to make them think, "We've got to meet this person."

Proofreading may not be glamorous, but it's essential. A typo can be the difference between landing an interview and landing in the reject pile. Read your cover letter out loud, have a friend review it, or use writing assistance tools. Do what it takes to ensure it's polished and professional.

Lastly, let's talk about the format. Yes, the content is king, but an unruly format can overshadow even the most compelling narrative. Stick to a simple, clean layout. Use a legible font (no Comic Sans, please), and ensure proper spacing. It's like dressing up for an interview – you want to look sharp, not flashy.

To wrap it all up, remember that your cover letter is essentially a personal sales pitch. It's your chance to humanize your accomplishments, add color to the numbers, and share your enthusiasm for both the role and the world of data science. Be genuine, be specific, and most importantly, be you. Because, at the end of the day, that's who they're looking to hire.

So, take a deep breath, let your personality and passion for data science shine through, and start writing. Your engaging, memorable cover letter could be the key to unlocking exciting new doors in your career. Best of luck!

Chapter 4:
Mastering the Data Science Interview Process

So, you've jazzed up your resume, penned the cover letter of the century, and now you've landed an interview for a data science position. Congrats! You're probably halfway between excitement and the urge to binge-watch "number crunching" tutorials while nervously nibbling on your pen. Fear not, intrepid data warrior, for mastering the interview process is less about memorizing Python libraries in your sleep and more about showcasing your analytical prowess and how well you play in the data sandbox with others. The data science interview is a beast of its own kind, blending technical grilling with behavioral probing, all while trying to convince a panel of humans that you, indeed, are the data whisperer they've been searching for.

First, let's talk about the types of interviews you might face. You've got your technical interviews, where it's showtime for your coding skills, and you prove you can wrestle data into submission. Think of it as a gladiator match but with keyboards. Then, there's the behavioral side of the Coliseum, where you'll weave tales of past projects, showcasing not just your technical skills but your ability to navigate the stormy seas of team dynamics and deadlines. This isn't about reciting your resume like it's the latest script for a blockbuster movie; it's about painting a picture of how you approach problems, collaborate, and occasionally make magic happen with a dataset and a couple of coffee-fueled nights.

Prepping for common interview questions is like training for a marathon - minus the actual running and more mental gymnastics.

Remember to share stories if you want a solid grasp of the technical concepts. Yes, stories. Humans love stories. They're like the secret sauce in your interview toolkit. "Tell me about a time when..." prompts are: Your cue to shine—transforming technical challenges and solutions into captivating narratives highlighting your creativity and resilience, occasionally and your heroic ability to save the day with a clever piece of code.

It's not just about flaunting what you know; it's about demonstrating how you think, learn, and grow. So, grab that pen you were nibbling on, jot down a few of your most epic data adventures, and let's get you ready to ace that interview and land the data science gig of your dreams.

Understanding Different Types of Interviews

So, you've polished your resume, nailed the cover letter, and landed an interview for a data science gig. Let's dive into the mystical world of interviews, shall we? Except it's not so mysterious once you break it down. In the realm of data science, interviews can come in various flavors, each with its unique twist and opportunity to showcase a different aspect of your mad skills. First, we have the technical interview, the beast about coding, algorithms, and sometimes, making you wonder if a blackboard has suddenly become your worst enemy. It's a rite of passage in the tech world. But hold your horses; we're not yet diving into the deep end of technical interviews. That's a story for another day.

Next on the docket are the behavioral interviews. Ah, the human side of things. If technical interviews are the swordplay, behavioral interviews are the diplomacy. Here's where you narrate your epic tales of collaboration and leadership, and perhaps that one time you saved a project from the brink of disaster with nothing but a clever pivot in strategy and a can-do attitude. These interviews are your moment to highlight the soft skills that complement your technical prowess. Because, as much as we love to geek out on data, we must remember the human element. After all, data scientists don't work in a vacuum (unless you're analyzing data on space vacuums, that is).

But wait, there's more! As we venture deeper into the jungle of job-hunting, it's worth noting that the format of these interviews can also vary wildly. From one-on-one interviews that feel like a cozy chat over coffee to panel interviews that might conjure up images of facing a tribunal, each format tests your mettle uniquely. While we won't get into the nitty-gritty of each format here (we've got to save some excitement for later chapters), it's crucial to understand the landscape. Whether decoding puzzles in a technical assessment or weaving compelling narratives in a behavioral interview, knowing what to expect is half the battle. So, sharpen those hard and soft skills and show these interviews who the boss is.

Technical Interviews

The technical interview is the infamous, sometimes spine-tingling, always mind-boggling stage of the data science job interview process. Don't sweat it too much. After all, if solving problems wasn't your jam, you wouldn't have decided to dive into the deep end of data science. So, let's unravel the mysteries of technical interviews together, shall we?

First, the technical interview is your golden opportunity to showcase your mad skills. It's not just about proving you can code; it's about demonstrating your problem-solving prowess, analytical acumen, and ability to swim in the vast ocean of data. It's your time to shine, showing off how you can turn data into decisions and decisions into actions.

Now, let's talk prep. You wouldn't run a marathon without training, right? (If you would, I wonder whether to be impressed or concerned.) Treat the technical interview like a marathon. Begin by brushing up on the basics: your programming languages of choice (Python and R are good pals in the data science world), statistical analysis, and machine learning concepts. Oh, and please, for the love of all that is binary, don't neglect your SQL. It's the bread and butter of data manipulation, after all.

But knowing your stuff is only half the battle. You've got to be ready to think on your feet. Data science technical interviews often include live coding challenges or take-home assignments designed to simulate real-world problems. Practice breaking down these problems into manageable chunks. Try to articulate your thought process as you go along. This helps you keep track of your progress and shows your interviewers how you approach a problem, which is pure gold in the interview world.

One aspect that gets overlooked is the importance of explaining your work clearly and concisely. You could be the next Einstein of data science, but if you can't explain your analysis to someone who thinks Python is just a snake, you will have a hard time. Interviews often include cross-disciplinary team members, so practicing explaining complex concepts in Layman's terms is invaluable. This demonstrates your technical expertise and ability to communicate effectively—a killer combo in the data science field.

If the word 'statistics' makes you want to run for the hills, it's time to face your fears. Data science and statistics go together like peanut butter and jelly. Expect questions that test your understanding of statistical theories and their application in real-world scenarios. Brush up on your knowledge of probability, regression, and experimental design. Not only will this help with the technical interview, but it's also handy for impressing people at parties.

Another hot tip: get comfortable with data visualization tools. Think of it this way: data visualization is the art of turning numbers into insights and insights into stories. And who doesn't love a good story? Being able to create meaningful and eye-catching visualizations shows your capacity to make data accessible to others, a skill that's worth its weight in gold.

Let's talk about machine learning. Yes, it sounds like something out of a sci-fi movie, but it's a fundamental aspect of data science. Familiarize yourself with different machine learning algorithms and understand when and why you would use one over the other. Interviewers may throw curveballs your way, asking you to distinguish between types or to explain the logic behind choosing a specific algorithm for a problem.

Remember the importance of understanding the business context. It's not all about the numbers and the code. Interviewers often look for candidates who can interpret data through the lens of business goals or challenges. Demonstrating that you can translate technical insights into business recommendations can set you apart from the competition.

I know what you are thinking. This is talk and no walk. So let me walk the distance and give you an example.

Scenario:

Imagine you're in a data science interview for a retail company. The interviewer presents a dataset containing customer purchase history, website interaction data, and demographic information. They ask you to analyze the data and provide insights to help the company improve its marketing strategies.

Approach:

Understanding the Business Goals:

Before diving into the data, you start by asking specific questions about the company's marketing objectives. You inquire about their target audience, current marketing strategies, and any challenges they are facing.

Data Analysis and Interpretation:

After understanding the business context, you analyze the dataset to identify patterns and trends. You uncover that a significant portion of the website traffic comes from a specific demographic group, but the conversion rate is low among this group.

Interpreting Insights in Business Terms:

Instead of just presenting the numbers, you interpret the insights in the context of the company's goals. You suggest that the low conversion rate could be due to a mismatch between the marketing messaging and the preferences of the identified demographic group.

Providing Business Recommendations:

Based on your analysis, you recommend tailoring the marketing content to better resonate with the identified demographic group. You propose A/B testing different marketing messages to gauge their effectiveness.

Highlighting the Business Impact:

Finally, you emphasize how implementing these recommendations could potentially lead to a higher conversion rate and increased revenue from the target demographic, aligning with the company's business objectives.

This example demonstrates how you can effectively merge data analysis with a deep understanding of business goals and challenges, showcasing your ability to translate technical insights into actionable business recommendations.

Definition of Conversion:

"Conversion is the intended action that a business or organization wants its audience to do. In this context of e-commerce, conversion frequently refers to achieving a specified goal, such as making a purchase, signing up for a newsletter, or completing a contact form on a website. The percentage of site visitors who take the targeted action is frequently used as a key performance indicator (KPI) to assess the efficiency of marketing campaigns or the user experience of a website."

So, here is the framework:

1. **Understanding the Business Goals**

2. **Data Analysis and Interpretation (trends and patterns)**

3. **Interpreting Insights in Business Terms**

4. **Providing Business Recommendations**

5. **Highlighting the Business Impact**

Practice makes perfect, or at least much better. Hunt down technical interview questions online, participate in hackathons, or tackle real-world projects. Getting your hands dirty with actual data will improve your skills and boost your confidence. Remember, confidence is vital. Walking into an interview feeling prepared can make all the difference.

Here's another piece of advice: stay curious. Data science is constantly evolving, with new tools, techniques, and theories emerging. Keeping up to date with the latest trends shows interviewers that you're not just looking for a job but passionate about the field. It shows that you're someone who will continue to grow and contribute long after the interview is over.

Last but certainly not least is the art of the follow-up. After your technical interview, take a moment to send a thank-you email. It's polite, but it also allows you to reiterate your interest in the role and the company. You can also briefly mention anything you forgot to say during the interview or clarify an answer you feel could have been better.

Technical interviews can be intimidating, but they are opportunities to learn and grow. You might nail some of the questions, and that's okay. What's important is showing that you're thoughtful, adaptable, and eager to face challenges head-on. So, go forth and show those technical interviews who's boss!

And remember, the worst technical interview is the one you didn't learn from. Each interview is a steppingstone, not just to your next job, but to becoming a better data scientist. After all, in the world of data science, every bit of experience counts. So, take a deep breath, believe in yourself, and dive into your following technical interview with confidence and a dash of humor. Who knows? You might enjoy the challenge.

So, here's to ace your technical interviews, learning something new with each one, and the exciting journey of a career in data science. See you on the other side!

Behavioral Interviews

So, you've made it past the resume screen, and now you're up against the behavioral interview beast. What's the deal with these, you ask? Well, imagine someone asking you to tell them about a time you did something great but also a time you messed up – and you must spin both in a way that makes you look good. Sounds fun, right? It's like trying to pat your head and rub your belly simultaneously. But fear not, our data science warriors, for we're about to dive deep into the do's and don'ts of these mind games.

First thing first: understand what the interviewer is after. They're not just trying to make you sweat for fun (well, mostly not). Behavioral interviews are designed to get a glimpse into your past behavior, which is often the best predictor of future behavior. They want to know how you've handled real-life situations, worked with others, solved problems, and adapted to change. It's like being a fortune teller, but instead of reading tea leaves, they're reading your past experiences.

Now, let's talk stories. Everyone loves a good story, especially your interviewer. When prepping for behavioral interviews, think of your career as a collection of blockbuster movies. You want to have a handful of go-to stories that showcase your skills, achievements, and lessons learned. These stories should have a clear beginning, middle, and end – or, as they say in the biz, a situation, task, action, and result (STAR). This method keeps you on track and ensures your answers are structured and impactful rather than rambling into oblivion.

One common mistake is thinking you can wing it. Trust me, you can't. Even the most charismatic folks need to practice their stories. You don't want to find yourself halfway through a tale only to realize it's more of a snooze-fest than a showstopper. So, practice out loud, in front of a mirror, to your cat, or even to your plant. Ensure your stories hit all the key points and keep your audience engaged.

But what about negative experiences? The dreaded "Tell me about a time you failed" question. Here's the thing – everyone fails, but not everyone knows how to turn a failure into a win. When crafting these stories, focus on what you learned and how you've improved since. This shows resilience and the ability to grow from mistakes, which, spoiler alert, are pretty essential qualities in data science.

Remember to tailor your stories to the job you're applying for. Just like you wouldn't wear a clown suit to a job interview (unless it's for a clown), don't bring irrelevant stories to the table. Highlight experiences that showcase the skills and qualities the job description emphasizes. It shows you've done your homework and can connect the dots between your past experiences and the role's requirements.

Non-verbal communication plays a massive part in how your stories are received. You could tell the most compelling story, but you might as well be reciting the phone book if you're mumbling into your chest or avoiding eye contact. Be mindful of your posture, make eye contact, and, for goodness' sake, remember to breathe. It's okay to take a moment to collect your thoughts. A thoughtful pause is better than filling every silence with "um" and "uh."

Questions? Yes, you should have some. Interviews are a two-way street, and showing curiosity about the role, team, and company culture is good. It demonstrates enthusiasm and a genuine interest in the position. Plus, it lets you catch your breath and learn something.

Handling curveball questions — those out-of-left-field, what-kind-of-fruit-would-you-be questions — with grace is also part of the game. The interviewer might be testing how you handle ambiguity or think on your feet. There's often no "right" answer here. Still, your response can showcase your creativity, problem-solving skills, and even your sense of humor.

Remember, interviews are as much about fit as they are about skills. Behavioral interviews allow you to show off your personality. Don't be a robot regurgitating rehearsed answers. Let your passion for data science and your unique personality shine through. After all, you're not just a collection of skills and experiences; you're a human being they'll be working with (hopefully).

Feedback can be your best friend. After your interview:

1. Reflect on what went well and what didn't.

2. If you have a trusted mentor or friend in the field, discuss your answers with them and get their take.

3. Use this feedback to fine-tune your approach for the next time.

4. Yes, there will likely be a next time, but each interview is a chance to improve.

Ah, rejection. It sucks, but it happens. If you don't land the role, it's not the end of the world (though it might feel like it for a bit). Seek feedback from your interview, learn from the experience, and move on. The right opportunity will come along, and you'll be even better prepared for it.

Finally, remember to follow up. A thank you note might seem old-fashioned, but it's a simple gesture that can set you apart. It shows gratitude and reinforces your interest in the role. Plus, it's another chance to remind them how great you are (as if they could forget).

In summary, attending a behavioral interview is all about preparation, storytelling, resilience, and a dash of personality. Keep your stories STAR-studded, practice your delivery, learn from your experiences, and don't forget to be human. You've got this, future data science star. Now, go knock their socks off.

Preparing for Common Interview Questions

So, you've landed an interview for a data science position. That's fantastic! But now comes the part that can tie your stomach in knots—prepping for those curveball questions they'll throw at you. Fear not! We're here to arm you with strategies and insights that'll make you so ready that you'll wish the interview was happening now.

First things first, let's talk about the technical questions. You've probably heard rumors of notorious coding challenges or statistical theory questions. The best way to tackle these is to ensure you're comfortable with your programming languages (Python or R, I'm looking at you) and have a solid grasp of statistical principles. Brush up on fundamental algorithms and data manipulation techniques and engage in mock coding interviews online.

But it's not all about coding and stats. Data science is as much about solving problems as it is about crunching numbers. Be prepared to discuss how you approach problem-solving. Think of a challenging situation you solved—maybe cleaning a particularly messy dataset or creating a model that was not behaving. How did you tackle it? What was the outcome? These stories stick in interviewers' minds.

Remember those behavioral questions? "Tell me about yourself" and "What's your biggest weakness?" These classics are classics for a reason. They give your interviewer insight into who you are beyond the resume. The STAR method (Situation, Task, Action, Result) is golden for these. It can help you structure your answers compellingly. Your 'biggest weakness' story ends with how you turned it into a strength, showcasing growth and self-awareness. That's the stuff they want to hear.

Oh, and the ever-popular "Why do you want to work here?" or "What interests you about data science?" For the love of data, do your homework on the company and the role. Be ready to get specific about their projects, values, or team dynamics that excite you. Avoid generic responses that could apply to any company. The more personalized your answer, the better. It shows you care.

Collaboration questions are also common. Data science isn't a solo sport. You'll be asked how you work in a team, deal with conflicts, or manage projects. Reflect on your experiences in team settings, particularly those involving multidisciplinary efforts. Highlight how you've communicated complex ideas effectively or navigated disagreements.

Expect to talk about your projects and experiences, too. This is not the time to be modest—lay out your achievements, the challenges you faced, and how you overcame them. But remember, honesty is key. If you inflate your resume, you'll get caught. Stick to the facts and let your genuine skills shine.

Questions about your learning process or how you stay updated with new technologies might also pop up. This is your chance to show off your passion for data science and commitment to continuous learning. Talk about the blogs you follow, the courses you've taken, or the projects you tinker with on weekends.

And hey, curiosity goes both ways. Prepare thoughtful questions to ask at the end of the interview. For example, inquire about the team's current projects, tools, or challenges. This will reflect your interest and enthusiasm for the role.

Another pro tip is to practice mock interviews. Practicing with a friend, mentor, or even in front of a mirror can boost your confidence. Please pay attention to what you say and how you say it. Body language speaks volumes. So, remember to smile, maintain eye contact, and keep the fidgeting to a minimum.

In truth, nerves are normal. But remember, the interview is as much about them getting to know you as it is about you evaluating if this role and company fit your career goals. You're interviewing them as much as they're interviewing you.

To summarize, crack open those books, refresh your coding skills, and line up your project stories. Dive deep into understanding the company and reflect on your desires and motivations in the data science field. Be sincere, be curious, and, above all, be yourself. That's the person they're looking to hire, after all.

And lastly, take a deep breath. You've got this. Landing the interview is already a huge win. Now go out there and show them why you're the data scientist they've been looking for!

Remember, preparation doesn't make perfect—it makes prepared. Being prepared is the best ace you can have up your sleeve. So, go nail that interview and step into the exciting world of data science. The future is waiting, and it's looking pretty data driven.

Chapter 5:
Real-World Case Studies and Projects

After surfing through the dazzling world of resumes, cover letters, and the thrilling roller-coaster of interview processes, you've made it here to the treasure trove of real-world case studies and projects. This isn't just any chapter; it's your golden ticket to showing off your skills in a way that will make potential employers do a double-take - in a good way. Think of it as your data science runway, where instead of strutting designer clothes, you're showcasing your sleek, well-executed projects and case studies that scream: 'Hire me!'

Now, diving into projects might seem a tad overwhelming at first. You might be wondering, "Where do I even start?" The secret sauce to winning over employers' hearts (and job offers) is cherry-picking projects that display your technical prowess and highlight how you can solve real-world problems. Whether predicting stock market trends or creating a model that can accurately suggest products to customers, the aim is to pick projects that resonate with the issues companies face today. And remember, the tale of how you tackled challenges during these projects can make for an epic story during interviews, showcasing your problem-solving skills and creativity.

And let's remember to learn from those who've already navigated the stormy waters of data science interviews and emerged victorious. There's no better way to prepare than by studying real-life cases of individuals who nailed their data science interviews. By dissecting what worked for them, from the projects they chose to discuss to how they articulated their thought process, you can glean insights into what employers are looking for. It's like having a behind-the-scenes pass to the data science job market, providing you with the intel needed to tailor your approach and projects in a way that resonates with interviewers. So, let's get cracking on those projects and case studies and turn the job hunt game in your favor.

Displaying Your Skills Through Projects

So, you've made it past the theoretical jungle and the treacherous terrain of technical skills. Congrats! But hold up; you're about to embark on a quest that separates the hopefuls from the hired: showcasing your skills through real-world projects. You've heard it a million times - experience is king. But how do you get experience without a job and a job without experience? Ah, the age-old chicken and egg scenario. Well, fret not because projects are your golden ticket.

Let's talk about the elephant in the room - projects can be anything from a fancy machine-learning algorithm that predicts stock prices to a simple data visualization of your monthly spending habits. The key isn't the complexity; it's the relevancy and what it says about you as a data scientist. It's like picking an outfit for your first date. You want to impress but also show you're a good fit.

Start with what interests you. Passion shines through, and trust me, interviewers can tell when you're genuinely excited versus when you're just going through the motions. Did a Kaggle competition capture your fancy? Or is there a pesky problem at your current job that could be solved with some data wizardry? There's your project idea.

Next, document your process like you're the next J.K. Rowling— well, perhaps without the magical creatures. The point is that storytelling is crucial. How did you approach the problem? What obstacles did you encounter, and how did you overcome them? This narrative is interview gold. It shows you're not just a coder but a thinker and a problem-solver.

Now, I know what you're thinking: "But I'm no Picasso. How do I make my project look good?" Fear not, friend. The beauty of data science projects is in the insights, not the aesthetics. A beautifully crafted dashboard is great, but clear visualizations and well-commented code can be just as impactful. Focus on clarity and simplicity. Remember, you're trying to communicate your findings, not dazzle with design.

Oh, and let's not forget about the power of collaboration. Group projects aren't just for school. They show potential employers that you can play nice with others, which, spoiler alert, is essential in most jobs. Working with others can help you tackle more complex problems and acquire new skills.

Let's address the elephant-sized question, "Where do I showcase these projects?" GitHub is your digital portfolio, where you can display all your hard work for the world to see (and, more importantly, potential employers). Make sure your repo is organized, your README file is detailed, and your commitment to the craft is evident.

While we're on the topic, don't dump all your projects on GitHub and call it a day. Curate your selection. Pick the ones that best showcase your skills and evolution as a data scientist. Think of it as your greatest hits album. You wouldn't include that song you wrote in five minutes in the shower, would you?

Another gem is blogging about your project experience. It's one thing to show your work; it's another to articulate the process, challenges, and learnings. Platforms like Medium or your blog are great spaces to expand on your projects and share your thought process.

This not only enhances your visibility but also underscores your communication skills.

Now, remember when I said to start with what interests you? Here's where it comes full circle. When you pick projects, you're passionate about, it becomes easier to talk about them. Imagine being in an interview, and the conversation shifts to something you're genuinely excited about. You'll light up, become more animated, and engage more deeply. That enthusiasm? It's infectious and can make a lasting impression.

But don't just take my word for it. Practice explaining your projects to a non-technical friend. If they get lost in the jargon or the significance of your work doesn't come across, you've got some refining to do. The ability to communicate complex ideas in a simple and engaging way is a superpower in the data science world.

Lastly, feel free to reflect on what didn't work. Projects that didn't go as planned or experiments that failed can be just as informative, if not more so, than your successes. What matters is what you learned from the experience and how you pivoted or persevered. It shows resilience, another trait high on an employer's wishlist.

Projects are not just about showing off technical chops; they're a multi-faceted showcase of your problem-solving skills, creativity, and personality. They provide a unique opportunity to make your resume come alive, tell your story, and demonstrate that you're not just another candidate – you're a data scientist ready to make an impact.

So, go forth and projectify your passion. Dive into data sets, wrestle with real-world problems, and emerge with a portfolio that showcases your skills and the journey of growth and learning you've embarked on. Remember, in the realm of data science interviews, projects are your best foot forward. It's time to make sure they shine.

And with the right projects under your belt, your next job interview could be the last one you'll ever need to prepare for. So, let's get cracking, shall we? The world of data is vast and full of possibilities, waiting for someone like you to unravel its secrets.

Learning from Successful Data Science Interviews

Have you ever heard someone say, "I crushed my data science interview by binge-watching 'Star Trek' the night before"? Probably not, and if you have, take it with a grain of salt. But let's beam up some wisdom from those who've boldly entered the interview room and emerged victorious. What's their secret sauce? Spoiler: It's not just about mastering Python or R; it's also about showcasing your Vulcan-like logic under pressure and your Captain Kirk-level confidence.

First off, remember that storytelling isn't just for kids or Netflix series. Successful candidates know how to spin a good yarn around their data project experiences. It's one thing to say, "I built a predictive model." It's another to explain, "I built a predictive model that identified potential customer churn, boosting retention rates by 15% and saving the company millions." See the difference? One tells what you did; the other paints a picture of your impact. Be the Picasso of your data science stories.

Let's discuss the obvious issue at hand—technical skills. Sure, being a wizard at coding is great, but showing you understand the why behind the code sets you apart. That is a valuable technical skill. Successful interviewees don't just regurgitate code; they explain their thought process, why they chose one method over another, and how it fits into the bigger picture. Think of it as showing your work in math class. Yes, the answer is essential, but how you got there is the real gold.

When it comes to the dreaded technical challenges, practice makes perfect. But here's a twist - don't just practice on your own. Find a buddy, a mentor, or a kindly stranger online willing to give you mock technical interviews. This helps you get comfortable speaking about your logic and prepares you for curveball questions. And let's face it, there's always a curveball.

Remember, soft skills are your secret weapon. You can code in your sleep, but how about teamwork? Can you handle feedback without crumbling? Successful candidates excel in these areas. They listen, communicate effectively, and show they're team players. After all, nobody wants to work with a genius who's a nightmare to interact with.

Preparation is vital, but over-preparation can be your downfall. You heard that right. Some candidates come in so scripted that they might as well be reading from a teleprompter. Be flexible. Be ready to pivot discussions and show your adaptability. Data science is never static, so why should your interview responses be?

Let's talk failures. They're inevitable, but they're also gold mines for learning. Successful candidates are open to discussing their failures. They embrace them, showcasing their problem-solving prowess and resilience. It's all about the comeback story. So, next time you face a 'Tell me about a time when you failed' question, remember it's your time to shine.

Networking isn't just for getting the interview; it's for acing it, too. Candidates who come recommended or have inside knowledge about the company's challenges through networking have an edge. They can tailor their responses, projects, and even questions to show they're a great fit not just technically but culturally, too.

Oh, and about those projects - they're your interview lifeline. Successful interviewees choose projects to showcase that are technically impressive and also relevant to the company or role they're interviewing for. It's like saying, "Not only can I do cool stuff, but I can do cool stuff that matters to you."

Have you ever heard the phrase, "Dress for the job you want, not the job you have"? Well, it's true for interviews, too. I'm not saying don a lab coat and goggles, but dressing appropriately shows respect and professionalism. It's the unspoken handshake before the actual handshake.

Feedback is a two-way street. Post-interview, successful candidates follow up to thank the interviewer and seek constructive feedback, even if they get the job. It shows a growth mindset and flatters the heck out of the interviewers. Everyone likes to be asked for advice; it's human nature.

Humor me for a moment, but visualization techniques work. Imagine nailing the interview, from your confident introduction to flawless technical explanation. It sounds woo-woo, but trust me, it sets a positive mindset. And a positive attitude is contagious; interviewers can sense it. You might not have them cheering, but they'll be mentally high-fiving you.

Lastly, curiosity didn't just kill the cat; it landed the cat a job in data science. Successful candidates are insatiably curious. They ask questions about the company, the team, upcoming projects, and the role itself. It shows engagement and a genuine interest in being part of the company. Plus, it turns the interview into a conversation, which is way less intimidating.

So, while there's no magic wand to ace every data science interview, learning from those who've traversed this path and emerged victoriously can give you a blueprint for success. Remember, it's not just about what you know but how you apply it, communicate it, and learn from it. Be the candidate that stands out not just for their technical prowess but also for their ability to fit within a team, tackle challenges head-on, and bring a fresh perspective. Now, go forth and conquer those interviews with the grace of a gazelle and the precision of a data scientist!

Chapter 6:
Negotiating Your Dream Job Offer

So, you've dazzled them with your technical prowess and charmed them with your problem-solving acumen. The interviews are behind you, and voilà, a job offer lands in your lap. It's tempting to do a victory dance and sign on the dotted line without a second thought, especially if it's a place buzzing around your dreams like a determined bee. But hold your horses—or, should we say your algorithms. The art of negotiation is the last crucial step between you and your dream data science job, and guess what? It's about more than just the numbers.

Evaluating the offer is where you need to channel your inner detective. Sure, a fat paycheck is great, but what about the work-life balance, the team dynamics, and the growth opportunities? Like a well-structured dataset, a good job offer is comprehensive and balanced. Consider all the variables. If the place is notorious for midnight oil burning but offers an astronomical salary, weigh it against your personal life and mental health. Remember, a job is a significant part of your life, not the whole plot. Also, does the role excite you? Will you jump out of bed each morning eager to face the challenge, or will it be a snooze fest? These are the questions you're going to want answers to.

Now, let's talk tactics. Negotiating is like trying to solve a Rubik's cube blindfolded. Still, it's more about understanding value—both yours and theirs. Don't just bark numbers; build your case. Why are you worth more than they're offering? Use your achievements and skills as leverage, not to mention the industry standard for someone with your background in data science. Be confident but not cocky, flexible yet firm. If done right, this dance can not only bump up your package but also showcase your negotiation skills—a big plus in any job. And remember, the goal here is to reach an agreement that leaves both parties victorious. So, take a deep breath, put on your game face, and let the negotiation games begin. Trust me, a well-negotiated offer is the cherry on top of your data science dream job.

Evaluating the Offer

So, you've blown everyone's mind with your incredible skills and charming personality, and voila, you've got an offer! First off, high-fives all around. Now, before you start celebrating by buying a new gadget or booking that dream vacation, let's take a moment to dive deep into what's on the table. Yes, I mean the job offer.

Let's be real: The excitement of getting an offer can sometimes cloud our judgment. It's like going on a first date and thinking about how to introduce someone to your parents before you even know their last name. So, let's put on our analytical hats (yes, the same one you wore during those data science interviews) and start dissecting that offer.

The salary is often the first thing we look at, and rightfully so. It's a big part of why we work, right? But don't just look at the number and think, "Sweet, that'll buy a lot of pizza." Consider the cost of living in the area, compare it with your current or previous salary, and think about future financial goals. Is the dough enough?

Benefits are the silent heroes of any offer. Health insurance, dental, vision, retirement plans, parental leave, etc., can significantly impact your overall satisfaction and financial health. Make sure to understand the details. What's covered? What's not? How much do you have to contribute from your paycheck? Remember, a healthy you is a happy you.

Now, let's talk about work-life balance. Are the working hours flexible or fixed? Can you work from home, or is it all about that office life? Think about your lifestyle and what works best for you. Also, consider the commute. A long commute can be a major buzzkill and can seriously eat into your personal time and wallet with travel costs.

Professional development opportunities are like the secret sauce to your career progression. Does the organization support learning and growth? Are there opportunities for training, certifications, or attending conferences? Staying up-to-date in the fast-evolving data science field is crucial, so you want to ensure you'll continue growing your skillset.

The company culture can make or break your work experience. Try to get a feel for the environment. Is it collaborative or competitive? Innovative or traditional? The vibe should align with your values and how you like to work. Sometimes, a great culture fit can outweigh other aspects of the job offer.

Consider the team you'll be working with. During your interviews, did you get a chance to meet potential colleagues? Did you click with them, or was there an awkward vibe? Remember, you'll spend a lot of time with these folks, so you must feel like you can collaborate and learn from them.

Career progression is another crucial aspect. What does the path forward look like at this company? Are there clear opportunities for advancement? You don't want to be stuck in a dead-end role without any chance of moving up the ladder. Make sure there's room to grow.

Job stability and company outlook are also critical. In the fast-paced world of tech, startups can be thrilling but risky. More significantly, established companies might offer more stability but less innovation and flexibility. Consider what's essential for you and where you see the company going.

And let's remember the impact of the work you'll be doing. Does the product or service excite you? Do you believe in the company's mission? Your work should feel meaningful to you. Otherwise, it's just going to be a long slog to retirement.

Lastly, consider any unique perks the company offers. It could be something as simple as free snacks or as extravagant as yearly company retreats. While these shouldn't be deal-breakers, they can sweeten the pot and show that a company values its employees' happiness and well-being.

Now, this seems like a lot to consider, and it is. But remember, this is your career and life we're talking about. It's worth evaluating an offer thoroughly to ensure it aligns with your values, career goals, and lifestyle.

If you're feeling overwhelmed, make a pros and cons list. Seriously, it's not just for deciding whether to binge-watch another season. List all the factors important to you in a job, and see how the offer stacks up. This can help clarify things and make a decision easier.

And remember, almost everything is negotiable. If the offer's elements need to meet your expectations, feel free to negotiate. We'll discuss negotiation tactics in the next section but know that it's okay to ask for what you believe you deserve.

So, please take a deep breath, and let's make sure that dream job offer is as dreamy as it seems. After all, you've worked hard to get to this point. You deserve a job that challenges you, pays you well, and makes you smile (almost) every morning.

Negotiation Tactics for a Better Package

So, you've aced the interview, crushed the technical questions like a grape, and now you've got an offer in your inbox. Before you start doing your victory dance around the living room, let's talk strategy.

Yes, I'm talking about the art of negotiation. Don't sweat it if you've never been in a haggling match over a flea market find; negotiating your job offer is a tad more sophisticated and, luckily for you, comes without the musty smell.

First thing's first, know your worth. Data scientists are in hot demand, and guess what? You're now one of those sought-after commodities. Do a bit of sleuthing on salary websites, network chats, or even ask around discreetly. Having a clear understanding of an appropriate range for your role in your specific area is crucial. You're not pulling numbers out of a hat; you're basing your counteroffer on cold, hard facts.

Never, and I mean never, jump at the first offer. It's like accepting the first slice of pizza from the box; hold out a minute, and you might get a bigger piece. Politely express your enthusiasm for the role - you're not playing hard to get, after all - but mention you'd like some time to review the offer. This is your chance to breathe, dissect the offer, and prep your counter like a data science ninja.

Your counteroffer shouldn't just be about the base salary. Think big picture. Maybe the company can't move much on salary, but they could possibly be flexible with signing bonuses, stock options, or work flexibility. Remember, your total package is not just your salary. It's the whole enchilada - benefits, perks, and other compensations that make your work life sweet.

Practice, practice, practice. Negotiating might not feel as natural as Python scripting, but with a bit of rehearsal, you'll get there. Try role-playing with a friend acting as your future employer. It might feel silly at first, talking to your pal as if they're the CEO of Big Data Corp, but getting comfortable with your pitch can make a world of difference.

When you make your counteroffer, be concise and confident. Highlight your skills, experiences, and the value you bring to the team -

yes, this is the time to toot your own horn, just make sure not to sound like a foghorn. It's about striking the right balance between assertiveness and politeness.

Avoid the trap of emotional negotiation. It's easy to get caught up in the moment, especially if you feel you're being lowballed. Keep it professional, stick to the facts, and remember, you're having a business conversation. They're not trying to insult you; it's just negotiation.

While salary is vital, it's not the end-all-be-all. Consider aspects like the company culture, growth opportunities, and the team you'll be working with. Sometimes, taking a slightly lower salary might be worth it if it means landing in a place where you can thrive and advance in your career. Think long-term.

Prepare to meet halfway. The goal of negotiation is for both parties to feel like they've won. If the company counters your counter, that's OK. It means they're playing ball. Be ready to compromise and find a middle ground that makes you both happy.

Document everything. Once you've reached an agreement, make sure it's all in writing. The details of your negotiation should be outlined in the final offer letter or contract. This is not just for bookkeeping; it's to ensure there are no misunderstandings about what was agreed upon.

Don't forget to express gratitude. Whether your negotiation ends with you accepting the offer or deciding to pass, being polite and thankful is key. The tech world can be small, and burning bridges is never wise. Who knows, you might cross paths with these individuals again down the line.

If the negotiation doesn't go your way, don't despair. Not every job out there is the right fit, and it's better to realize this during the negotiation phase than three months into the job. Keep your chin up, learn from the experience, and dive back into the job hunt with new insights and strategies.

Last but not least, remember that negotiation is a skill, and like any skill, it gets better with practice. Whether you're negotiating your salary, deciding who does the dishes, or haggling at a garage sale, each experience builds your confidence and finesse.

Securing your dream job in data science is about more than just technical chops; it's about advocating for yourself and ensuring you're compensated fairly for your skills and contributions. Approach the negotiation table with preparation, confidence, and a dash of tact, and you'll be well on your way to a package that reflects your true value in the data science realm. And once that's done, feel free to do your victory dance. You've earned it.

So go forth, negotiate like a pro, and remember – your expertise in data science is your leverage. Use it wisely, and don't sell yourself short. The perfect offer doesn't just come knocking; sometimes, you have to negotiate your way in. Good luck!

Chapter 7:
Transitioning Into Your New Role

So you landed the job—congrats! You're now a bona fide member of the data science world. The ink on your contract is barely dry, and you're probably feeling excitement and a bit of terror. That's normal. The first 90 days in your new role will be a whirlwind of learning, meeting new faces, and trying to remember where the coffee machine is. This period is crucial; it's your chance to soak up as much as possible, prove your worth, and set yourself up for long-term success. But remember, it's okay to ask where the bathrooms are more than once—nobody expects you to memorize the office blueprint on day one.

Now, let's talk about the art of continuous learning and career growth because, in data science, if you're not moving forward, you're essentially going backward. The field is constantly evolving—with new tools, techniques, and theories popping up faster than mushrooms after rain. Staying on top of these developments will ensure you remain a valuable asset to your team and help you carve out a niche for yourself. Get comfortable being uncomfortable because learning in data science is a never-ending journey. Embrace it, and you'll create innovative solutions to problems you didn't even know existed a few months prior.

Finally, remember that transitioning into your new role is more than just sharpening your technical skills. It's also about integrating into your team, understanding the company culture, and building relationships. Be curious, be eager, and don't be afraid to be the one who brings donuts on a random Tuesday. Little things can make a big difference in how you're perceived and open doors to opportunities within the organization you have yet to consider. So go ahead, dive in head first, and start making waves. Who knows? You might just become the office's next data science superstar.

The First 90 Days

Welcome to the jungle, or as some may call it, your new data science role! If you've made it this far, pat yourself on the back, dance, and prepare to embark on a thrilling rollercoaster. The first 90 days are crucial; think of it as your runway before takeoff. It's not just about proving you're smart enough for the job (spoiler: you already did that by getting hired) but also about integrating yourself into the team, understanding the company culture, and starting to make an impact.

First things first, let's talk about the basics. You will want to show up on time, dress appropriately, and ensure your coffee doesn't spill on your laptop. But beyond these common-sense tips lies the real golden nuggets of starting your job on the right foot. It's like navigating a minefield where every step forward counts, and the occasional misstep could send you flying back to the starting line.

One of the first things you should focus on is understanding the lay of the land. Every company has its own unique culture and way of doing things. Some are as laid-back as a cat in the sun, while others are as structured as a military operation. Should you accept it, your mission is to figure out where your new gig falls on this spectrum. Observe, listen, and ask questions. Remember, no question is too silly if it helps you understand your new environment better.

Building relationships is key. You're not a lone wolf but part of a pack now. Get to know your colleagues, understand their roles, and figure out how you can support each other. Trust me, being the lone genius in the corner cubicle won't do you any favors. It's like being stranded on an iceberg – impressive to look at from a distance but isolating. Reach out, grab coffee with teammates, and get involved in projects or meetings, even if they don't directly relate to your role. This is your chance to shine as a team player!

Here's where the rubber meets the road: setting your goals. Within your first few weeks, having a one-on-one with your boss is essential not just to bond over your shared love for obscure Python libraries but to understand what success looks like in your new role. What are the expectations, and how can you exceed them? It's like mapping out your treasure hunt—without a map, you're just wandering around, hoping to stumble upon gold.

Let's remember to learn. Yes, you're expected to bring your A-game and stellar skill set to the table, but there's always room for growth. Dive deep into any new tools or software that's part of your job description. Be proactive and ask for training if you need it. It's like you've been given a new video game to master – sure, you could wing it, but wouldn't you rather know all the cheats and shortcuts?

Mistakes – let's talk about them. They're inevitable, like tripping on an untied shoelace. What matters is how you handle them. Own up to them, learn from them, and move on. Remember, every mistake is just a stepping stone to becoming the data science ninja you're destined to be.

Feedback is your friend, not your foe. Seek it out actively. It might sting a little, like ripping off a Band-Aid, but it's essential for growth. Think of it as tweaking your code – painful at the moment but incredibly satisfying once it's done.

Communication is key. Your data models might be complex, but your communication style should be different. Please keep it simple, whether it's a technical presentation or a casual chat by the water cooler. Your goal is to be understood, not to impress with jargon.

Remember to celebrate small victories. Did you finally crack that pesky algorithm? Did you manage to make your first presentation without shaking your voice? These are wins, my friend, and they deserve a little happy dance. It's these moments that will fuel your journey.

Be patient with yourself. Rome wasn't built in a day, and neither is a data science career. You'll face challenges, and there will be days when you feel like trying to solve a Rubik's Cube in the dark. Keep at it; perseverance is key.

Finally, make sure to carve out time for reflection. After your first month, take a step back and review. What's working? What's not? Adjust your strategies accordingly. It's like debugging your career path – iteration leads to perfection.

Remember, transitioning into your new role is a marathon, not a sprint. Keep a positive attitude, stay curious, and don't be too hard on yourself. Every day is an opportunity to learn, grow, and inch closer to being the data science guru you aim to be.

As you progress through your first 90 days, remember these tips. They are steps and leaps towards making your mark in your new role. Embrace the challenge, enjoy the journey, and let's turn those data dreams into reality!

So, there you have it—your survival guide for navigating the murky waters of your first 90 days. Arm yourself with knowledge, a splash of humor, and a dash of humility, and you'll not just survive; you'll thrive. Here's to your success in the data science world—may your data always be clean and your insights sharp!

Continuous Learning and Career Growth

So, you've nailed the interview, charmed the socks off the hiring panel with your dazzling wit and breathtaking analysis, and you're now officially a card-carrying member of the data science workforce. What's next, you ask? You don't just want to be part of the scenery; you're aiming to become one of those legendary figures in the office that everyone, even the office cat, looks up to for wisdom and insight. The secret, my friend, is continuous learning and relentless pursuit of career growth.

First, let's get something straight: the data science landscape is as stable as a bowl of Jell-O on a high-speed train. New technologies, tools, and techniques pop up faster than you can say "machine learning algorithms." This means that resting on your laurels and becoming complacent with your current skill set is akin to career suicide. But fear not! This ever-evolving terrain is also brimming with opportunities for those willing to keep learning and adapting.

One way to ensure you're constantly growing is by setting aside weekly time for learning. Can't spare an hour a day? No problem. Even dedicating a single afternoon a week can propel you miles ahead of the competition. Utilize online courses, webinars, and tutorials to learn new programming languages or statistical methods. Remember, in data science, staying au courant is not optional; it's essential.

Then there's the power of side projects. These are not just a great way to learn new skills; they also add some serious sparkles to your resume. Dive into datasets that pique your interest, or better yet, start a project that solves a problem for your current organization. Not only will this showcase your initiative and ability to apply your skills practically, but it might also catch the eye of higher-ups.

Participation in the community is also a massive booster for learning and career growth. Attend workshops, conferences, and meetups. You'll gain insights from leading experts in the field and start building a network that can open doors to opportunities you never knew existed.

But what about those soft skills you've heard so much about? Yeah, they matter—a lot. As data gets bigger, communicating complex analyses becomes increasingly critical. Hone your presentation skills, practice writing clear and concise reports, and, if the thought makes you queasy, seek out opportunities to speak publicly. These skills can set you apart in a tech-heavy field.

Mentorship is another golden key to unlocking your potential. Finding a mentor within your organization or industry can provide invaluable insights, advice, and perspectives you might have yet to consider. It's a two-way street; mentoring someone else can reinforce your knowledge and hone your leadership abilities.

Let's not forget the importance of feedback. It's the breakfast of champions, after all. Seek it out actively, and don't just wait for your annual review. Ask colleagues and superiors for input on your projects and presentations. It's a fantastic way to identify areas for improvement and accelerate your learning curve.

For those looking for leadership roles, consider the value of understanding the business side of things. Data scientists who grasp the commercial implications of their work are like gold dust. They can bridge the gap between technical and non-technical teams, making their insights and analyses indispensable for driving business decisions.

And, in the spirit of keeping things spicy, why not learn something entirely out of left field? Dabble in an area unrelated to data science. Whether it's philosophy, design thinking, or even improv comedy, you'll be surprised at how these seemingly unrelated skills can provide fresh approaches to problem-solving and creativity in your day-to-day work.

Advancement doesn't always mean climbing the corporate ladder in the traditional sense. It can also mean deepening your expertise in a niche area of data science that fascinates you. Becoming the go-to expert for a specific domain makes you irreplaceable. It allows you to shape the direction of your career with more autonomy.

Naturally, all this talk of growth and learning leads to the subject of career progression. Be proactive about seeking out new challenges and opportunities within your organization. Don't shy away from expressing your career aspirations to your manager. Be prepared to outline how you plan to add value to the team and the company.

Ultimately, remember that career growth in data science is not just about mastering the latest algorithm or analytics tool. It's about continually evolving, both professionally and personally. It's about staying curious, seeking out challenges, and not being afraid to fail—because that's where the real learning happens.

So, there you have it—the roadmap to becoming not just a data scientist but a data science legend. It's not an easy journey, but with continuous learning and a focus on career growth, it's definitely an exciting and rewarding one. Now, go forth and conquer those datasets with the ferocity of a thousand suns!

Conclusion

Well, here we are at the culmination of our quirky yet informative journey into the realm of data science job interviews. Suppose you've paddled along from the early pages. In that case, you've now surfed through the craggy coastlines of data science essentials, dove into the depths of your toolkit, and emerged, hopefully, as a more polished, interview-ready version of yourself. Let's not mince words: the road to landing that dream data science job can be as perplexing as a poorly documented piece of code. But fear not, we've tried to unpack those complexities with a blend of humor and guidance that has steadied your nerves.

The landscape of data science is ever evolving, and so are the skills required to shine in this field. Remember, mastering technical skills like Python, R, SQL, and others is just one side of the coin. The flip side is honing those soft skills – communication, problem-solving, and the like – that can make you stand out. Never underestimate the power of a well-articulated thought or the ability to unravel complex problems with the most straightforward solutions.

A finely tailored resume and a cover letter that speaks volumes about your passion for data science are your tickets to that coveted interview call. Make them count. Once you get to the interviewing stage, remember that every question, whether technical or behavioral, is an opportunity to showcase your knowledge, personality, and approach to problems.

The real-world projects and case studies we discussed should serve as a testament to your capabilities. They're not just bullet points on a resume but stories waiting to be told, each highlighting different facets of your expertise and character.

Negotiating your job offer might feel like trying to optimize an algorithm for an outcome where you've got limited control over the variables. Yet, understanding your worth and the value you bring to the table is crucial. The tactics we've covered are your parameters; adjust them wisely to land an offer that fairly compensates your skills and contributions.

Transitioning into a new role is an adventure. The first 90 days are crucial for making a mark and setting the tone for your tenure. Embrace continuous learning because, in the world of data science, the only constant is change. Keep updating your toolkit with new programming languages or techniques and enriched experiences from every project you undertake and every problem you solve.

My final piece of advice? Stay curious. Curiosity is the fuel that will drive your growth in this field. It will push you to ask questions, seek answers, and continuously improve. Whether digging deeper into a dataset, mastering a new data visualization tool, or understanding the underlying psychology behind user behaviors, let your curiosity lead the way.

Networking might not have been a chapter in this book, but let's not undervalue it. Connect with peers, mentors, and leaders in data science. Each interaction is an opportunity to learn, share, and grow. And your next job offer might come from a casual conversation at a meetup.

Remember, rejection is not the end of the road but a mere detour. If a job interview doesn't go as planned, dust yourself off, analyze what went wrong, and apply what you learned to your next interview. Persistence, paired with continuous learning, is vital.

As you close this book (or close the tab on your e-reader or the audio app you are listening from), take a moment to reflect on how far you've come. Preparing for data science interviews is no small feat, and you've taken significant strides toward achieving your career goals. Celebrate your progress and keep building on it.

And finally, always remember why you chose data science in the first place. Whether it was the allure of unraveling complex datasets, making data-driven decisions, or impacting the world in meaningful ways, let that passion keep you motivated.

In the spiraling world of data, the opportunities are as vast as datasets waiting to be analyzed. Your unique skills, curiosity, and persistence are your ticket to unlocking these opportunities. So, keep coding, querying, and, most importantly, dreaming. The following excellent data science innovation is yours to discover.

To everyone who's been part of this journey, thank you for letting me be a part of your preparation. I can't wait to see where your skills and ambition take you in data science. Now, go out there and ace those interviews!

Appendix A:
Additional Resources for
Data Science Career Success

So, you've gulped down every chapter, absorbed the tips like a pro, and even chuckled at the odd joke or two (you did, didn't you?). But let's face it, the data science world is vast, like "scrolling through your social media feed" vast. And while we've covered the A-Z of nailing that job interview, there's always more to learn. Enter Appendix A - a treasure chest of resources to keep you sharp, inquisitive, and, let's be honest, downright unbeatable in the data science arena.

Books That Pack a Punch

First, hitting the books (not literally; we love books) is a great way to keep your brain ticking. Add titles like "Data Science for Dummies" for a basic refresher or "Naked Statistics" to make sense of the world through a data lens. Also, "The Signal and the Noise" by Nate Silver is a must-read for one to appreciate the art and science of prediction. Trust me, you'll get insights wrapped in stories that are so engaging that you might just forget you're learning.

Online Courses That Don't Yawn

Next up, online courses. Hear me out; some can be as exciting as watching paint dry, but there are gems out there. Platforms like Coursera, edX, and Udacity offer courses designed with industry leaders like Google and IBM. Whether you're diving into Python, wrestling with R, or just looking to buff up your machine-learning prowess, there's a course for you. Plus, you can often join for free (because who doesn't love free stuff?).

Catch Up on Podcasts and Blogs

Are you not in the mood for reading or courses? Podcasts and blogs are your best friends. Plug into "Data Skeptic" for your weekly dose of skepticism infused with data science, or "Not So Standard Deviations," to hear professionals casually debate over statistical tools and news. Blogs like Towards Data Science on Medium slingshot complex concepts down to Earth, making them digestible for mortals like us.

Networking without the Awkwardness

Remember, it's not just what you know but who you know. And before you envision awkward networking events, think digital. LinkedIn is for more than just when you're job hunting. Engage daily, connect with industry leaders, and participate in discussions. Twitter is also a gold mine for real-time trends, job openings, and the occasional data science meme from fellow nerds.

Keeping Your Tools Sharp

Last but not least, staying hands-on is critical. Sites like Kaggle not only let you participate in competitions but also provide a playground to apply what you've learned to real datasets. It's the perfect way to test your skills, learn from others, and even win some bragging rights (or job opportunities, but bragging rights sound cooler).

Wrapping up, think of this list as your personal data science gym membership. It'll keep you fit, but it's up to you to use it. So, dive in, explore, and remember : curiosity didn't kill the cat in the world of data science; it got it a job.

www.ingramcontent.com/pod-product-compliance
Lightning Source LLC
Chambersburg PA
CBHW071609200326
41519CB00021BB/6929